*A Gateway Devotional*

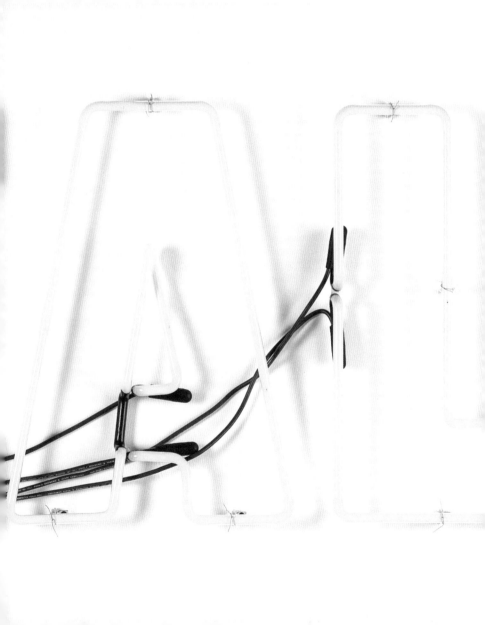

## *REAL: A Gateway Devotional*

**Written by** *Robert Morris, Niles Holsinger, Ben Pirtle, Josh Morris, S. George Thomas, Jelani Lewis, Karen Hageman, Tim Ross, Preston Morrison, Matthew Hernandez, Zach Neese, Courtney Watkins, Elaine Fisher, Craig Terndrup, Kyle Fox, Chelsea Seaton, Kam Hunt, Jan Greenwood, Mark Jobe, Troy Wierman, Raul Cabrera, Mark Harris, Marcus Brecheen, Sion Alford*

**Editorial Director** *Shea Tellefsen*
**Senior Editor** *Daniel Hopkins*
**Copy Editor** *Georgette Shuler*
**Contributing Editor** *Stacy Burnett*
**Creative Director** *Shane Dennehey*
**Art Director & Designer** *Tim Lautensack*
**Production Designer** *Perri Adcock*
**Photographer** *Adam Fish*

Requests for information should be addressed to:
*Gateway Publishing, 2250 E Continental Blvd, Suite 150, Southlake, TX 76092*

# CONTENTS

# AUTHENTIC

# LIFE

# PREFACE

vangelism has always been near and dear to my heart. When I first went into ministry, I was a traveling evangelist and would share my personal testimony at church services almost every week. While I don't travel nearly as much now, I've never stopped witnessing and sharing my story with people I meet.

Have you ever shared your story with someone? Maybe you've tried sharing it with a friend, but you weren't sure what to say. The truth is, it's easy to share your story and this devotional will help you understand how.

*REAL* focuses on equipping and inspiring you to effectively communicate the story of the Gospel and your faith by living a ***relevant, engaging, authentic life***. As you read through these devotions, you'll see that these words are the key ingredients to being a good witness and sharing your story with others.

My hope is that through this devotional you'll be able to see just how easy and powerful it is to share your story and lead people to the Lord! The reason the great evangelists have led so many people to the Lord is because they've had a lot practice. But you don't have to have the gift of evangelism to be an effective witness. You may not have the gift of intercession, but as a Christian you still need to pray. In the same way, as a Christian, you still need to be a witness and share your story with others.

I believe that if you make this devotional part of your daily life over the next 28 days, you'll be inspired to build the kingdom by living out *REAL*.

*Robert Morris*

**Pastor Robert Morris**

# RELEVANT

*Having obvious significance upon;*
*pertinent; or relating to the matter at hand.*

# *DAY 1*

# RELEVANT FISHERS

By Robert Morris

*And Jesus, walking by the Sea of Galilee, saw two brothers, Simon called Peter, and Andrew his brother, casting a net into the sea; for they were fishermen. Then He said to them, "Follow Me, and I will make you fishers of men."* Matthew 4:18–19

y son James is a fisherman and has been since he was a young boy. When he was about four years old, he started learning a lot about fishing by watching fishing shows on Saturday mornings. One of my favorite memories of James was when he was seven years old and we were fishing at a trout pond in Colorado. On our way to the pond, we stopped at the store for some bait. James carefully chose the bait he wanted to use and as he placed it on the counter, the man behind the cash register said, "This won't work!" Undeterred, James told him he wanted it anyway.

As we walked out to the pond, James went over to an area where no one else was fishing, and within minutes he caught nine trout! You could see groups of men around the pond begin to move over to where James was fishing. Many of them asked what bait he was using and went back into the store to buy the same kind. One man even asked James for fishing advice, and once James taught him how to cast his line, he started catching fish. Remember, James was just a little kid! But boy, was he a good fisherman!

Have you ever thought about why Jesus chose fishermen to be His disciples? The more obvious choices might have been gifted preachers or maybe even politicians with a lot of influence. But no, He chose rugged, outdoor-oriented men who knew how to go after something and catch it. Think of what this implies: He gave the work of the ministry to normal, everyday, working people.

He's called us all to be fishers of men, but many of us have never caught any fish. It's surprisingly simple to do. All you need is the right bait and to cast your line in the right location. If you're wondering, *What is the right bait?*, I have some good news for you: *you already have it*. Bait is any story about God's goodness. It could be your salvation experience or a story about how God changed your life. A friend of mine shared a story with me about his daughter whose eyesight was healed. He and his wife prayed for her for months, and one morning she woke up with perfect eyes! Do you know what he did next? He emailed this story of God's goodness to all of his clients, and this led to people giving their lives to Jesus!

So, what's your story about God's goodness? Are you ready to share it with everyone around you? Don't be afraid. Just put some bait on your hook and cast it, then you'll start catching some fish.

### PRAYER

*God, I thank You for Your goodness. Remind me of stories of Your goodness so I can share them with others, and remove any fear I have about sharing. In Jesus' name, Amen.*

## WHAT IS THE HOLY SPIRIT SAYING TO ME?

## FOR FURTHER STUDY

*Ephesians 4:12; John 21:1–14*

# *DAY 2*

# TWO HUNDRED BROWNIES

By Niles Holsinger

*"If I could speak all the languages of earth and of angels, but didn't love others, I would only be a noisy gong or a clanging cymbal. If I had the gift of prophecy, and if I understood all of God's secret plans and possessed all knowledge, and if I had such faith that I could move mountains, but didn't love others, I would be nothing. If I gave everything I have to the poor and even sacrificed my body, I could boast about it; but if I didn't love others, I would have gained nothing." 1 Corinthians 13:1–3 (NLT)*

anette was a seventh-grade teacher I met during an outreach to one of our local middle schools. When we met, she was eight days away from completing her first year of teaching. It wasn't her first career. Actually, it was her third. She explained to me that when the Lord began to speak to her about leaving her high-level job in the banking industry and going back to school to become a teacher, she thought it was a mid-life crisis. She was in her mid-forties and had an established reputation in a great field but realized something was missing. She wanted a career that would allow her to spend the rest of her life building others up.

On the first day of school, she looked at her students and said, "This year, you will love me and sometimes you will hate me—but I will only love you." Now, if you've ever been around a seventh-grade student, you know that statement would be put to the test very quickly. I asked her if she still felt the same way about her students now that the school year was coming to a close, and she answered, "You know what I did on Memorial Day? I made 200 brownies from scratch and wrapped them up to give to each of my students. I wouldn't have done that if I didn't still love them."

Lanette was excited that the school year was coming to an end, but she was even more excited about the news that her teaching contract had been renewed for another year, and she would be back with the students she loves.

When I think of her, I think of what my life would look like if I was completely driven by love. Could I do what she did? Could I change the entire course of my life to love people better? Could my eyes see with a love that "will cover a multitude of sins" (1 Peter 4:8)? When I think of Lanette, I am reminded of Jesus.

Can you imagine the feelings of the woman caught in adultery in John 8 when she looked up into the eyes of Jesus and experienced forgiveness and peace instead of judgment? And the leper in Matthew 8; think of his shock when Jesus touched him (Jews were not allowed to touch lepers according to Leviticus) and healed him of a disease that had no cure.

If we want to be relevant to the world around us, it begins with us loving the world around us. We need more people like Lanette because we need more people like Jesus. What will you do to show the love of Jesus to the world around you today? You may not need to make 200 brownies, but a simple act of love and grace can make a huge difference in someone's life.

### PRAYER

*Lord, I pray that You would open my heart to love the way You love. To see people not for their faults or shame, but for their value. I pray that when people meet me, they only see You. In Jesus' name, Amen.*

## WHAT IS THE HOLY SPIRIT SAYING TO ME?

## FOR FURTHER STUDY
*John 13:34–35, Mathew 22:37, 39–40*

DAY 3

# A DANGEROUS MISSION

*By Ben Pirtle*

*Then He said to them, "Follow Me, and I will make you fishers of men."*

Matthew 4:19

One day while Jesus was choosing His disciples, He asked several fishermen to do something out of the ordinary. He told them to follow Him so He could make them fishers of men. He then led them on a three-year expedition in search of broken and disenfranchised people who needed to be rescued from the grip of their sin.

In Luke 19, as Jesus and His disciples and followers passed through Jericho, they came across Zacchaeus, a wee little man who climbed up in a sycamore tree to see Jesus. Zacchaeus was a wealthy con man who acquired his fortune by cheating and stealing from his own people. He was hated for his dishonesty and immoral lifestyle. But to Jesus, he was a soul worth fishing for.

In this story, Jesus stops His procession when He notices Zacchaeus, and He says to him, "I want to come and hang out at your house today." This shocked the religious people because Zacchaeus was essentially the enemy. As Jesus walked away from His familiar followers to speak to this rebellious outcast, He knew something His followers hadn't yet realized: fishing for broken people requires going out of your comfort zone to where they can be found.

When Jesus made this shift from the safety of His friends to the house of the rejected, something drastically changed. Zacchaeus welcomed Him in, turned from his sin, and then repaid four times the amount to all from whom he had stolen! He received Jesus' forgiveness and then became a blessing to those whom he formerly abused!

It is at this very point of the story when Jesus said, "'Today salvation has come to this house .... For the Son of Man has come to seek and to save that which was lost.'" Jesus didn't leave heaven to come sit in a safe zone surrounded by admirers. Jesus came on a dangerous mission to bring salvation to people who were destined for hell.

Here's where it gets dangerous for us!

We are called to follow Jesus—not simply into His Father's house, the Church, but also into the spaces that are occupied by the enemy. This is where the hurting people live. In your neighborhood and your school. They are hanging out at your job and at the gym. They congregate in restaurants, athletic fields, and shopping malls. It is time to answer the call from Jesus, "Follow Me, and I will make you fishers of men." Where must we follow Jesus? Outside of our comfort and into the dark corners of the world where the lost are begging to be found!

### PRAYER

*Father, give me the courage to take the light that I have received in Your house to the dark world, and use me to represent Your love to the lost! In Jesus' name, Amen.*

_____

_____

_____

_____

_____

_____

_____

_____

_____

_____

_____

_____

_____

_____

_____

_____

_____

_____

_____

FOR FURTHER STUDY

*Mark 16:15; Acts 20:24; Romans 1:16*

DAY 4

# YOU HAVE THE ANTIDOTE

*By Josh Morris*

*"I have given them your word. And the world hates them because they do not belong to the world, just as I do not belong to the world. I'm not asking you to take them out of the world, but to keep them safe from the evil one. They do not belong to this world any more than I do. Make them holy by your truth; teach them your word, which is truth. Just as you sent me into the world, I am sending them into the world. And I give myself as a holy sacrifice for them so they can be made holy by your truth."*

*John 17:14–19 (NLT)*

Imagine for a moment that you live in a place that is infested with venomous snakes. People around you are constantly dying from snakebites. One day you are bitten and when death is closing in, someone reaches down, picks you up, and gives you a drink. This drink contains anti-venom—not only does it save your life but also protects you from the future threat of snakes. It gives you permanent resistance to them. The same person also tells you where to find a lifetime supply of anti-venom and encourages you to share it with others.

If this imaginary scenario really happened, how unbelievable would it be if you were to walk around keeping the anti-venom to yourself? People would be suffering all around you and instead of helping them with the lifesaving anti-venom, the only thing you'd offer is that you've heard of another place that doesn't have any snakes, which does nothing to relieve their current suffering.

This analogy shows how some Christians have chosen to live their lives. Many of us walk around knowing the antidote to death and rest contently knowing how great heaven *will* be, rather than bringing the kingdom of heaven to a world that is suffering right now. When people are living in hell on earth, they need more than a promise of a pain-free future—they need help *now*. In today's passage, we see clearly that God sent us to earth just as Jesus was *sent* to earth. What was He sent here for? To save people—to freely pass out anti-venom!

Each of us has a mission here on earth and that mission is people. Who can you tell this week about the anti-venom that God freely gave you? Being in the world and not of it simply means you are a citizen of another land, and no matter how short your time is here on earth, you are fully present and engaged in what God is doing. We have been called here by God, so let's focus on the task set before us and accomplish the Great Commission that Christ has given us. Share it freely, with everyone!

### PRAYER

*Lord, thank You for saving me and giving me eternal life in heaven, but please help me remember that I'm still on this earth, and it's my job to share Your love and truth so you can save others. Give me the courage to be bold and share the gospel with people. In Jesus' name, Amen.*

## WHAT IS THE HOLY SPIRIT SAYING TO ME?

## FOR FURTHER STUDY
1 Peter 2:11–12; Philippians 3:20

DAY 5

# WHO'S MY NEIGHBOR?

By S. George Thomas

*"So which of these three do you think was neighbor to him who fell among the thieves?" And he said, "He who showed mercy on him." Then Jesus said to him, "Go and do likewise."* Luke 10:36–37

One day, a lawyer came to Jesus asking, "What shall I do to inherit eternal life?" Jesus responded, "What is written in the law?" Without hesitation, the lawyer rattled off: "Love God with all your heart, soul, strength, and mind. And love your neighbor as you love yourself." Jesus told him he should go and do exactly that, but the lawyer wanted clarification. "And *who* is my neighbor?" he asked. In other words, he said: Tell me who I *have* to love and who I *don't* have to love. Who do I have to accept, and who can I reject?

Instead of answering directly, Jesus told a story about a man who set out on a journey from Jerusalem to Jericho. But it was much more than just a story. Everyone listening to Jesus that day knew the road wasn't one you wanted to take after dark, because it was notorious for bandits. Sure enough, the man was attacked by robbers and thrown into a ditch to die. Eventually, a priest came riding by, but he angled across to the other side of the road to avoid him. The priest was followed by a Levite—another spiritual leader—who hurried by as quickly as possible.

31

Then Jesus introduced a Samaritan as the hero of the story. It was revolutionary because the Jews *despised* Samaritans. But when this Samaritan came upon the wounded man, he was moved with compassion. He cleaned the man's wounds, placed him on his own donkey, and took him to an inn and paid for it.

Jesus asked the lawyer, "Who do *you* think was a neighbor to the man who was beaten?" The lawyer couldn't even bring himself to say, "The Samaritan." Instead, he mumbled, "The guy who showed mercy." "That's right," Jesus replied. "Now go and do the same."

So what's the difference between the priest, the Levite, and the Samaritan? It all comes down to compassion. When he saw the wounded man, the Samaritan didn't say that the man "should have known better." No, he picked him up and brought him to a place of healing.

Ask yourself today, "Who's my neighbor?" It's those who've been robbed by the bandits of the world—fear, despair, grief, pain, poverty, disease, hate, hopelessness, misery—then left for dead. Everyone has experienced this at some point. No one is exempt. Do we keep our distance? Or will we allow our hearts to be moved with compassion?

Ask God to soften your heart to those around you—toward your neighbors, co-workers, and even strangers. Ask Him to stir up a love and compassion within you for them *and* their needs. Ask Him to give you the courage and wisdom to walk with them and offer them hope and life.

## WHAT IS THE HOLY SPIRIT SAYING TO ME?

## FOR FURTHER STUDY
Luke 10:25–37; Mark 12:31

*DAY 6*

# COMMON GROUND

By Jelani Lewis

*... I have become all things to all men, so that I may by all means save some. I do all things for the sake of the gospel, so that I may become a fellow partaker of it.* 1 Corinthians 9:22–23 (NASB)

I have one more question for you, if you don't mind," said the deacon who sat across the table from me at the diner. We had spent the last hour getting to know each other over eggs, bacon, and a side of perfectly cooked grits. He continued, "I've noticed since you've become the Frisco Campus pastor, there's been an influx of African-Americans at our campus. How can we make African-Americans feel more comfortable here?"

I have to be honest. That was absolutely *not* the question I expected to conclude our breakfast conversation. However, after internally regaining my composure,

my first thought was, "Thank You God for confirming my suspicions that the congregation was becoming increasingly more rhythmic in worship." Secondly, I was tempted to leap over the table and chest bump him like we just scored the game-winning touchdown against the Packers.

I settled, however, for immediately thanking him and then providing a few suggestions. I thanked him, not just because I am African-American and I appreciate the consideration. I thanked him because I am a believer and his question was about much more than race. His question was about how we make the gospel attractive to everyone regardless of color, culture, or class.

Paul wrote in 1 Corinthians 9:22, "I have become all things to all people, that by all means I might save some." In the three verses prior, the apostle claimed at various times he had become like Jews, Gentiles, and ... well ... weaklings, among other things. He declared he'd done everything short of sin to connect with people. Why? For the sake of the gospel!

In a culture saturated with separation, disagreement, and division, how do we mimic the intentionality of Paul? How do we find common ground so people can be found by Christ? I would like to suggest three ideas as a starting point: *look up*, *lay down*, and *lean in*. Look up means when we meet someone, we ask God to help us see them the way He does, through His lens of love. Lay down suggests we ask God to help us lay down our own personal biases, our preferences, and the priority of our own culture to fully embrace a kingdom culture. Finally, leaning in speaks to intentionally engaging in conversation with people to gain perspective. This encompasses asking questions like, "What is your perspective on_____?" and "How do you feel when_____?"

When we, as believers, see people the way Jesus sees them and appreciate and listen to their stories, we inevitably make it easier for people to embrace an even grander story, the story of God. After all, we truly do have common ground between us. The ground is level at the cross.

## PRAYER

*Father, thank You for the gospel, which is the power of salvation for all who believe. Today as I connect with people, will You help me look up, lay down, and lean in so people come to know You? In Jesus' name, Amen.*

## WHAT IS THE HOLY SPIRIT SAYING TO ME?

## FOR FURTHER STUDY
*1 Corinthians 10:31–33; Romans 1:14–16; Acts 10*

*DAY 7*

# WHAT'S ON YOUR MIND?

By Karen Hageman

*Guard your heart above all else, for it determines the course of your life. Avoid all perverse talk; stay away from corrupt speech. Look straight ahead, and fix your eyes on what lies before you. Mark out a straight path for your feet; stay on the safe path.* Proverbs 4:23–26 (NLT)

A while back I got an email from a woman who saw something I posted online. She was going through a very difficult situation similar to mine. I could completely relate to her feelings of shame and isolation. She thanked me and expressed how grateful she was to stumble across my post. It helped her not feel so alone. We later met up for coffee, and I was able to encourage her even more. This made me think about how much influence we really have through social media.

More and more people are using this type of network to connect. One of the benefits is it's a quick and easy way to communicate with so many people. It helps us keep in touch with family and friends we may not see or talk to very often. Unfortunately, there can be a lot of negativity as well. This technology platform has made it possible for us to hide behind our computers and post about anything and everything, including inappropriate or hurtful comments that have the power to ruin relationships.

However, if we follow what it says in Proverbs 4:24 ("Avoid all perverse talk; stay away from corrupt speech."), we can choose to walk a different path. We can be a positive influence everywhere we go and that includes the social media world. The key for us is being kind, authentic, and compassionate as we share our stories and interact with others.

Every time I log in to one of my favorite social media websites, I'm asked the same question: *What's on your mind?* I often post about my daily life and struggles. I love sharing what God is doing in my life. I'm able to encourage those around me and be encouraged. It's a great way to start a conversation. Many times I find that someone else is experiencing the same struggles I am. Life is rarely *picture* perfect, and it's reassuring to know we're not alone. God comforts us in our troubles and gives us the opportunity to comfort others (2 Corinthians 1:4). This creates an atmosphere of vulnerability and honesty with one another, which can then lead to healing.

Today, I encourage you to pray about how and what you communicate on social media. Our words can bring life or death. Think twice before you click on that *Post* button. Is it going to tear someone down or lift them up?

## PRAYER

**Dear Lord, thank You for the opportunity to share Your love with the world. Let my words glorify and be pleasing to You. I want to honor You in all I do. In Jesus' name, Amen.**

## WHAT IS THE HOLY SPIRIT SAYING TO ME?

## FOR FURTHER STUDY

*Psalm 19:14; 1 Corinthians 16:13–14; 1 Thessalonians 5:11*

# ENGAGING

*Tending to draw favorable attention or interest; attractive; pleasant; winning; charming.*

DAY 8

# THE SALT OF THE EARTH

*By Robert Morris*

*"You are the salt of the earth; but if the salt loses its flavor, how shall it be seasoned? It is then good for nothing but to be thrown out and trampled underfoot by men."* Matthew 5:13

Years ago, I was buying a car and really hit it off with the salesman. We had a great time talking about everything from hunting and fishing to fast cars. By the end of the transaction, we felt like old friends. That's when he asked me what I did for a living. When I told him I was a pastor, he looked stunned. "You've got to be kidding me!" he said. "You're not like *any* pastor I've ever met."

We decided to go to lunch later that day, and he shared his story with me. When he was growing up, he became friends with a boy at school whose father was a pastor. This boy was mischievous, and one day he convinced my friend to help him break into the church and ransack a room just for fun. When the pastor found out who did it, he was embarrassed. He didn't want his son to look bad so he blamed it on my friend and then kicked him out of the church in front of the entire congregation. It was the first and only time my friend ever went to church.

I told him I was sorry he had met a bad pastor all those years ago. We decided to meet again, and after a few more lunches, he accepted Christ as his Savior.

In Matthew 5:13, Jesus tells us we are the salt of the earth. Salt is a preservative and keeps things from decomposing. We are living among spiritually dead people, so by being the salt to others, we're preserving lives so they can hear the gospel and be saved. Without "spiritual salt," our society would die.

Salt also causes things to taste better. Pretend with me for a moment the gospel is a steak. We're the salt that helps it taste good. In the same way, when people come around us, they should be asking, "What is that taste? It's so good!" And it's because we're giving them a taste of God!

But Jesus goes on to caution us in this verse that if salt becomes bad and loses its flavor—its influence—it's not good for anything and should be thrown out. The first pastor my friend met was bad salt and made the gospel taste bad. But once my friend experienced good salt, he wanted to know Jesus!

When people are around you, what do they taste? Are you making God taste good or bitter? Are you making them hungry and thirsty for Him? If you want to be good salt, you need to stay close to Jesus and be purified by His word. That's all it takes to let people taste and see that the Lord is good.

## PRAYER

*Lord, thank You for making me salt to a world that needs to be preserved by the good news of the gospel. Help me to keep my flavor and be the good salt that will make others want to know You more. Thank You, Lord, for putting people in my life who I can influence for the kingdom. In Jesus' name, Amen.*

## WHAT IS THE HOLY SPIRIT SAYING TO ME?

_____

_____

_____

_____

_____

_____

_____

_____

_____

_____

_____

_____

_____

_____

_____

_____

_____

_____

_____

## FOR FURTHER STUDY
*Psalm 34:8; Romans 1:21*

**DAY 9**

# PROXIMITY TO CHRIST

By Tim Ross

*So we are Christ's ambassadors; God is making his appeal through us.*
*We speak for Christ when we plead, "Come back to God!"*

2 Corinthians 5:20 (NLT)

Have you ever felt out of place in the world around you? I'm sure that's how Daniel felt when the Israelites fell under the rule of the Babylonian king Nebuchadnezzar. Daniel, Shadrach, Meshach, and Abednego were taken as captives and brought in to learn about and enhance Babylonian culture with their intellect, so they could one day take positions in the king's court. They were basically given full-ride scholarships to Babylon University. And at BU, they learned the language, culture, history, politics, and creed of the kingdom.

They became completely engaged with the culture, but because of the integrity and fidelity they had with God, they were not influenced by it. Instead, they influenced it in a way that caused them to continuously be promoted. By the end of their education, the king found them to be even better than his own wise men, and he relied upon Daniel to interpret many of his dreams.

So how did they become fully immersed in this new culture while not being swallowed up by it? The answer is hidden in plain sight. They never fell in love with any of it, but they stayed in love with God.

49

In our world today, we're faced with a similar problem. We are surrounded by a corrupt culture, and many Christians choose to withdraw from it. However, that's not what Jesus did. When He walked the earth, He was constantly engaging with people—sinners, prostitutes, lepers, and others that religious leaders thought He should avoid. People take that to mean that Jesus *hung out* with sinners, but that's not the case. Because of His influence, *sinners* wanted to hang out with *Him*.

Anytime Jesus would go to the house of a sinner—take Zacchaeus, for example—His disciples went with Him. They were there because they were close with Jesus—not because they wanted to hang out with sinners.

We, as disciples of Jesus, are called to influence culture. That might mean engaging with a corrupt world. How do we keep from falling in love with the culture of the world? Take a look again at the way the disciples spent time with sinners—they stayed close to Jesus. Always ask yourself, "Where am I in proximity to Christ?" Allow the Holy Spirit to speak to you, and as you go out into the world, remain close to the One who can use you to help it.

*PRAYER*

*Holy Spirit, give me the boldness to be a bright light in a dark world. Allow me to have the grace to fill uncommon places with Your love. In Jesus' name, Amen!*

## WHAT IS THE HOLY SPIRIT SAYING TO ME?

_____

_____

_____

_____

_____

_____

_____

_____

_____

_____

_____

_____

_____

_____

_____

_____

_____

_____

_____

## FOR FURTHER STUDY

_Daniel 1; Acts 4:29; Acts 10:38_

*DAY 10*

# "YOU WANT TO USE MY LIGHT?"

> by Preston Morrison

*"You are the light of the world. A city that is set on a hill cannot be hidden. Nor do they light a lamp and put it under a basket, but on a lampstand, and it gives light to all who are in the house. Let your light so shine before men, that they may see your good works and glorify your Father in heaven."* Matthew 5:14–16

There is an underground cave in Northern Arizona our family found several years ago. We were driving through a forest having a good old-fashioned Morrison family adventure when we unexpectedly came upon it. Were we completely unprepared to explore it? Yes. Did we decide to do it anyway? Of course! It was our sense of adventure that drew us to it.

As we approached this unassuming hole in the ground, the closer we got, the more I realized this was going to be a pretty serious undertaking. There were other people exploring it as well; some had harnesses and backpacks, but everyone had flashlights. We, however, did not. We decided to go in and try the first 100 feet to get an idea of how cold, dark, and difficult it would be. But before we even made it 100 feet, it was so dark we couldn't see each other. Only when another climber would pass by us with a light could we see each other or where we were going.

As it was now quite obvious, due to the rising tension level of several in our group, we simply were not going to be able to make this journey happen without light. We decided to climb out and come back when we all had lights. Before we made it out, a man and his two sons noticed we had no light to travel by and said, "Hey, you want to use my lights? We've got three cheap lights from Walmart you can have. There's no way you guys could do this cave without them." Of course, I immediately responded saying, "How dare you offer me a light to more easily travel this dark place safely! Get away from me and take your light with you!" Okay, okay, you know I didn't actually say that. I'm trying to make a point. Of course, I was beyond grateful for his offer. The only reason we were able to explore the cave was because he gave us his light.

Sometimes I think we Christians tend to forget just how valuable light is in a dark place. Some of us are so afraid to be the light God has called us to be because we are afraid it will offend those around us. That cave was the darkest place I have ever been. Kind of sounds like the state of the earth now, right? The next time you see someone trying to move forward in complete darkness with no light, offer them yours. They'll be grateful you did.

## PRAYER

*God, please give me a heart that yearns to notice and help those walking in darkness. Give me the boldness required to stay bright in the darkest of places. In Christ's name, Amen.*

## WHAT IS THE HOLY SPIRIT SAYING TO ME?

## FOR FURTHER STUDY

*John 8:12; Ephesians 5:8*

DAY 11

# THE LIE OF PERFECTIONISM

By Matthew Hernandez

*"And a voice came from heaven: You are my beloved son; with you I am well-pleased."* Mark 1:11 (CSB)

With everything going on in our world today, I often find myself saying to the Lord, "God, we need You." One day recently, I whispered those familiar words and almost instantly I felt the Holy Spirit whisper back: "Well, I need *you*."

That moment changed everything for me.

What I realized was that God has given all of us influence, and He wants us to put action behind that influence. You use your influence by being willing and available to be used by God. As followers of Jesus, our role is to simply pursue Him with everything we are. Our obedience today will propel us toward how God will use our influence tomorrow.

However, many of us feel we aren't ready to be used by Him. The lie we often tell ourselves is that we have to reach a certain point in our relationship with Jesus to be ready. It's easy to get caught up trying to reach the unattainable goal of perfection in order to be influential for the kingdom. As long as we believe that lie, we can never rest in God's grace.

The truth is your influence is greater than you could ever imagine—especially when you live from a place of grace. When you live *from* grace, and don't strive to reach perfection, there's an attractiveness in that. People take notice, and what they see isn't us at all anyway. It's the good news that Jesus Christ is alive in us.

So, the question is: *how* are you using your influence? If you're like me, you have the potential to overcomplicate things. I can overcomplicate the folding of a bathroom towel so it's not far-fetched for me to overcomplicate a question that has a simple answer. Our tendencies to constantly strive and hustle to prove our influence are ineffective and exhausting. True influence happens when we realize we have nothing to prove and just obey and pursue Jesus as a son or daughter and invite others on the journey with us.

Today, I hope you realize the influencer you truly are. Right here and now. And may you hear the words of your Creator whisper to you: "This is my beloved child in whom I am well pleased." I encourage you to walk with that boldness, confidence, and peace today.

### PRAYER

*God, thank You that I can live my life from a place of confidence because of who You are and who You've called me to be. Help me to use the influence You've given me to give You the glory. In Jesus' name, Amen.*

## WHAT IS THE HOLY SPIRIT SAYING TO ME?

## FOR FURTHER STUDY

*John 14:12–14; Mark 16:14–18*

*DAY 12*

# PINCH POT PRIESTS

By Zach Neese

*But you are a chosen people, a royal priesthood, a holy nation, God's special possession, that you may declare the praises of him who called you out of darkness into his wonderful light.* 1 Peter 2:9 (NIV)

was supposed to be writing this devotion today. Deadline looming, I was feeling the pressure of the clock when I heard a sweet little voice behind me, "Daddy, will you play with me?" This explains how I ended up with clay all the way to my elbows, making pinch pots and Barbie plates in the backyard with my daughter Nora. "Daddy, I'm hungry" led to sandwiches with my son Sam and an intriguing conversation about the relative merits of certain Lego sets. "Daddy, I threw up four times" put me on the couch beside my daughter Judah, then at the doctor's office, then the pharmacy, and finally on my knees praying for her as she slept fitfully on the couch.

Each of these statements is like a little prayer, a simple expression of my children's needs. Each looked like a detour from my "mission" but was in fact a gift that allowed me to connect with my kids. When you connect with people, you also minister God's love to them. You connect heaven and earth, which is our true calling.

This calling to minister and connect is as old as humanity. Adam was created to connect God and creation. Walking with God, Adam ministered to His great, expansive heart. Then, walking in the garden, Adam ministered to the world God entrusted him with. As long as Adam ministered to God and creation, earth was a paradise in perfect relationship with God.

Of course, Adam fell and Jesus was born to carry the calling. Jesus' life was spent in continuous connection with His Father and connecting with hurting people—ministering to their diseases and heartaches. Ultimately, He shed His own blood to heal and seal the broken relationship between heaven and earth. Jesus is the living connection between the two.

The Bible calls this ministry the priesthood, and it is the honor of every believer to: connect with God, connect with people, and connect the two to each other. It doesn't require a master of divinity degree, and you've already been ordained by God Himself. You are called to steward the relationship between God and people. And so am I.

So excuse me, but I've got some priestly business to attend to. It's bedtime and I have six kids to pray with. That may sound like a mundane mission, but it is my greatest privilege to minister to their hearts and teach them to minister to God's heart—to steward their growing relationships with their heavenly Father. Pinch pots and prayers, sandwiches and doctor visits, Legos and consistent kindness—the details of life are the sacraments of our priesthood.

## PRAYER

*Father, thank You for reminding me that I am both Your child and a priest. Stay close to me today and show me how I can minister to Your heart. Give me opportunities to connect with people and to minister Your love to them—even in the mundane routines of life. As I do these two things, I pray that through Your Son, Jesus, You would connect every one of those people to Yourself. Now guide me to carry Your love and Your presence into my world. In Jesus' name, Amen.*

## WHAT IS THE HOLY SPIRIT SAYING TO ME?

_____

_____

_____

_____

_____

_____

_____

_____

_____

_____

_____

_____

_____

_____

_____

_____

_____

_____

_____

_____

## FOR FURTHER STUDY

_Revelation 1:5–6; 1 Peter 2:5; Hebrews 6:19–20; 1 Corinthians 6:19_

*DAY 13*

# REACH OUT

By S. George Thomas

*Moved with compassion, Jesus reached out and touched him. "I am willing," He said. "Be healed!"* Mark 1:41 (NLT)

A s a gifted bass-fishing pro, Sonny made a great living touring and competing on ESPN. He was well on his way to becoming a millionaire until he got caught up in a horrible drug addiction and began to sell off all his things—his house, boat, Harley—everything.

Sonny wound up homeless, living on the streets of Las Vegas. For eight months, he woke up every morning and washed people's car windows. Most days, the only thing he'd ever say was "Thank you" as people gave him a tip. Later in the day, he'd hop on a bus, ride across town to buy drugs, and come back to where he slept in a field beside a church.

Sonny didn't want *anything* to do with God, but one day, he walked into the church because he heard he could get a shower, food, and some clean clothes. It had been three months since his last shower, and he stunk horribly. Yet, when he walked through the doors of the church, a woman named Michelle—a soccer mom—looked directly at Sonny and said to him, "You look like you need a hug."

He looked at Michelle and said, "You don't want to hug me." She said, "No, you look like you need a hug." Despite the fact that he smelled awful, Michelle walked up to Sonny and embraced him. Looking in his eyes, she said, "Jesus loves you."

Thinking back to that moment, Sonny says, "I hadn't been hugged in months. With all the street preachers I had encountered, all the tracts people had given me, and all the 'Christian stuff' I'd seen in my life, nothing prepared me for *that* moment of genuine human contact." As he looked Michelle in the eye, something cracked in his heart.

Sonny took a shower, got some clothes, and checked out a Bible from the church's library. A few weeks later, he got on his knees and prayed, "God, I'm done. I don't know how I'm going to deal with this addiction, but I surrender my life to You."

Now, Sonny is drug-free, married, and a business owner. He's also making a positive difference as an advocate for helping the homeless in Las Vegas. And it's all because a soccer mom gave him a hug.

The Gospels tell us whenever Jesus encountered someone in need, He didn't just passively stand by and offer encouraging words. He always responded by *actively* reaching out and touching their lives, whether physically, emotionally, or spiritually. And He calls each of us to follow His example and do the same—to be His hands and His feet to those we come in contact with each and every day.

When it comes down to it, that's all "outreach" really is ... it's simply reaching *out*. Imagine what kind of difference *you* can make if you just allow God to use you to reach out to those in need around you!

## PRAYER

*Jesus, I want to reach out to those around me and love them as You would love them. I want to be like You. Show me ways I can practically love people every day. In Jesus' name, Amen.*

## WHAT IS THE HOLY SPIRIT SAYING TO ME?

## FOR FURTHER STUDY
*Mark 10:13-16; Matthew 20:29-34*

# *DAY 14*

# FOUND IN HIM

By Courtney Watkins

*Yet indeed I also count all things loss for the excellence of the knowledge of Christ Jesus my Lord, for whom I have suffered the loss of all things, and count them as rubbish, that I may gain Christ and be found in Him, not having my own righteousness, which is from the law, but that which is through faith in Christ, the righteousness which is from God by faith.* Philippians 3:8–9

We all have defining moments. Those times we're faced with a choice of how to see the world, and I remember mine so vividly. I'd been married for about four years and we were living in a small second-story apartment. My oldest daughter was just 14 months old and I had recently given birth to our second child (crazy, right?). My husband worked three jobs just to make ends meet and to complicate things even more, we only had one car. As you can imagine: small children + small apartment + financially struggling + limited adult interaction = a challenging season of life.

I felt trapped, but even more than that, I felt as if I had no purpose. I'd always worked either in ministry or a job that I felt "useful" in. I remember thinking to myself, *What happened to me? Is this my lot in life forever? Will I only be wiping noses and changing diapers the rest of my life?* But then came my defining moment.

As I sat folding laundry in my living room one morning, the Lord spoke so clearly to me. He asked, "If your situation never changes, will you still love Me?" That stunned me for a minute. I stopped folding the tiny baby clothes in my hands and had to seriously ponder that question. But even as I considered it, I felt something within me rise to His challenge. With tears in my eyes I said, "Yes, Jesus. I will love You even if this situation never changes. Even if I never get to *do* anything else, I will still choose You every day."

Isn't the Lord so sweet in how He speaks to us? He knows exactly what we need to hear that will heal the deepest places of our hearts. I didn't even know I was struggling with my identity, but when He spoke those words to me, it touched that very issue. My sense of worth and value were tied up in the things I felt like I could accomplish in life when all He was wanting was for me to be found in Him.

Three months later, we moved into a three-bedroom house and were the proud owners of a second car that someone gave us because the Lord told them to. Little did I know that a simple mindset change would make way for a physical change.

So many times we think our identity is tied to the amount of influence we have. When in reality, it's the opposite. When we truly know *who* we are, then our influence will be a natural outflow of that identity. He cares more about our hearts than He does about what we *do* for Him. At the end of the day, it's all about how well we love Him and His people.

## PRAYER

*Father, I put my trust and hope in You. I thank You that You love me and care more about my heart than everything else. Please root out any areas where I have put my identity in anything other than You. Help me to see myself the way You see me. I love You, Jesus! In Jesus' name, Amen.*

## FOR FURTHER STUDY
*Colossians 3:1–3; Jeremiah 1:5; Psalm 139:14*

# AUTHENTIC

*Genuine; real; trustworthy; reliable; that which can be believed or accepted; not counterfeit or false; true to its type.*

REAL

*AUTHENTIC*

DAY 15

# IT'S PERSONAL

By Robert Morris

*"But you shall receive power when the Holy Spirit has come upon you; and you shall be witnesses to Me in Jerusalem, and in all Judea and Samaria, and to the end of the earth."* Acts 1:8

I magine for a moment you and I are coworkers. We work in the same office building and there's a common area where people go to take a break and eat lunch. One day, I come into the common area, see a chair next to you, and ask, "May I sit here?" We strike up a conversation and talk about which departments we work in and how long we've been with the company. I say, "You know, I'm very grateful to be back at work because I was out sick for a while. I had an incurable disease that got progressively worse—to the point I couldn't talk or walk. I was completely bedridden. My family heard about a new drug the Food and Drug Administration was testing, and because it wasn't covered by my insurance, they raised the money to cover the cost. The drug worked and now I'm totally cured! That's why I'm happy to be back at work!"

Now if this had really happened, would you think I was trying to convince you of something or shove my beliefs down your throat? Of course not! It wouldn't be offensive to you because I was merely telling you what happened to me. I wasn't trying to convince you of anything. I was simply sharing my story with you.

Witnessing to people is much the same. You don't need to argue or persuade people, you just need to share your personal story. You see, being a witness is one of the easiest things for Christians to do. If you believe otherwise, the enemy has deceived you with fear, insecurity, or some type of false illusion. Witnesses are people who accurately communicate their experiences—what they have personally seen and heard—and every Christian should be a witness. In fact, every Christian is a witness. The question is, are you a good one or a bad one?

Some witnesses "plead the fifth" and stay silent, while others share compelling, eye-witness accounts. The disciples' testimonies were strong because they were personal. They literally walked with Jesus and watched Him change lives everywhere He went. He even changed their lives, and if you're a Christian, He's changed your life too.

When you share with others the way God has changed your life, there's a powerful truth that cannot be argued. So, whom will you share your story with today?

## PRAYER

*Lord, help me to be a good witness. I want to share the story of how You've changed my life in a loving way. Show me divine opportunities to share Your truth. In Jesus' name, Amen.*

## WHAT IS THE HOLY SPIRIT SAYING TO ME?

_____

_____

_____

_____

_____

_____

_____

_____

_____

_____

_____

_____

_____

_____

_____

_____

_____

_____

_____

## FOR FURTHER STUDY
1 John 1; Matthew 5:16; Psalm 40:9–10

DAY 16

# REAL AUTHENTICITY

By Elaine Fisher

*And they have defeated him by the blood of the Lamb and by their testimony.*

*Revelation 12:11 (NLT)*

I clearly remember the night I sat across the table from some family friends, who were great mentors to me. I was away from the Lord, and they shared a word from God with me they had received several years prior that confirmed my exact situation. In that moment, I heard the Lord say, "I want you!" I broke down and surrendered everything to Him. This is just a small part of my testimony that I tell often, and through it I've seen people give their lives to the Lord or change the way they were living because of its authenticity.

The night of that dinner I shared everything I was going through with my mentors. I was real, open, and completely honest. As soon as I finished, I told them they couldn't help me through this situation because I was just "too bad." Without missing a beat, they told me about the power of being authentic and bringing things to the light, which massively influenced how I tell my story.

Although there are times it's appropriate to share lots of details, the enemy sometimes tries to tell us that if we don't tell every detail to everyone, we aren't being *authentic*. That is a lie from the enemy. The Bible tells us that we don't need to share every detail because in doing so, we actually bring glory to the wrong thing. We only need to share enough to set the context, and then put the focus on bringing glory to Jesus.

Being authentic means being genuine. My story is unique to me, and we are each wired to share our stories. Being genuine in sharing that story will help give others hope, clarity, and awareness, but it also reminds us of what God has brought us through and that He continues to change us. When we share our stories, we remember how faithful God is, how much He loved us in a difficult season, and how He came through for us at just the right time. In remembering our stories, we remind ourselves that the same God who stood by us then will be standing by us again this time. Being authentic redeems our minds to remember who God is in our lives.

Take a moment today and remind yourself of different times God has come through for you. And in each moment of remembrance, watch your faith grow stronger. Then, I challenge you to share your story with someone and watch as their faith is strengthened by your authenticity.

## PRAYER

*Lord, remind me today of who You are. Build my faith so I can go out and be an authentic voice for You. Thank You for being a faithful God, in whom I can continually trust, for You never change. In Jesus' name, Amen.*

## WHAT IS THE HOLY SPIRIT SAYING TO ME?

## FOR FURTHER STUDY
*Acts 26; 1 Peter 3:15; Philippians 1:6–7*

REAL

*AUTHENTIC*

*DAY 17*

# AMBASSADORS FOR CHRIST

By Craig Terndrup

*Now then, we are ambassadors for Christ, as though God were pleading through us: we implore you on Christ's behalf, be reconciled to God.*

*2 Corinthians 5:20*

id you know that there are hundreds of United States ambassadors around the world right now? All of them have been appointed to represent our country wherever they go. And no matter where they are, because of diplomatic immunity, they are subject only to the laws of the United States. It truly is an honor to be an ambassador, and each one is a loyal public servant who must be secure enough in their position to speak truth to power. You and I are a different kind of ambassador—and though we reside on the earth, we are representatives of Jesus Himself.

The apostle Paul calls himself an ambassador for Christ, and in today's verse, Paul tells us it's our job as Christians to speak the truth, so others can know God. Paul did this everywhere he went. In fact, he was sent to prison for it, and even there he says: "praying always ... that I may open my mouth boldly to make known the mystery of the gospel, for which I am *an ambassador in chains*; that in it I may speak boldly, as I ought to speak" (Ephesians 6:18–20).

Being a representative for Christ may not land you in jail as it did for Paul, but it does carry a significant weight. When we speak, we speak on behalf of our King. We step into every situation with the full authority to represent the heart of Jesus, and we've been commissioned to share the message of the gospel. That is the role that we fill every day of our lives.

Right now, wherever you are, I encourage you to proclaim, "I am an ambassador of Christ." Your home is an embassy of heaven. Know that you have been sent to your workplace to reveal the reality of the kingdom of God, and you serve as an ambassador to your generation. In Jesus' name, you have great authority and a mandate to speak the truth in love to everyone you meet. So go out today and bring the kingdom of God with you wherever you walk.

## PRAYER

*Father, thank You for giving me authority as Your ambassador. Help me to speak Your truth everywhere I go. In Jesus' name, Amen.*

## WHAT IS THE HOLY SPIRIT SAYING TO ME?

_____

_____

_____

_____

_____

_____

_____

_____

_____

_____

_____

_____

_____

_____

_____

_____

_____

_____

_____

## FOR FURTHER STUDY

*Ephesians 6:20; 2 Timothy 3:16–17; John 17:6–8*

# DAY 18

# I AM QUALIFIED

By Kyle Fox

*"Whatever He says to you, do it."*

John 2:5

A venti black coffee and a bathroom break. That's all I wanted as my wife and I hurried into the Huntsville, Texas, Starbucks for a quick pit stop during a long road trip.

And then as I rushed into Starbucks, God pointed to someone I should talk to. *"But God! I'm technically still on vacation!"* You would have thought I was a five-year-old just asked to clean his room by the way I responded. In the time it took the barista to pour my coffee, I told God all the reasons why I should not talk to this person.

"He's going to think I am weird." "He probably wants to be left alone." "We need to get back on the road." And last, but not least: "What could I possibly say to this person that might help him?" I fought it—*hard*. We made it to the car when I turned around and went back inside.

I awkwardly sat down at the guy's table and asked how I could pray for him. I'll never forget the look of relief on his face. He told me he went there that morning to pray and shared that he had anxiety about a decision he had to make. Not only did I pray with him, I also shared that my wife and I had walked through what he was facing. In that moment, God used a stranger from North Richland Hills to remind this man he was not alone. God even told me to mail him a particular book a couple weeks later.

Looking back, it wasn't my insecurity or excuses that almost kept me from approaching him; it was doubting my qualification.

Moses felt far from qualified when God told him to lead the Israelites out of Egypt. There's a well-known quote, "God doesn't call the qualified, He qualifies the called." We tend to think of qualification in a broad sense: extensive training, career experience, or an advanced degree. What if we walked in confidence knowing God uniquely qualifies us for every situation in which He places us?

You know that *nudge* you feel in those moments? What if that nudge is a direct result of someone else's prayers? What if the only distance between a stranger and their breakthrough is the distance between you and that person? What if, in that moment, God chose you to bring a little bit of heaven into their situation? Our feelings of doubt can disable us. Feelings lie to us. We are at our best when we stop relying on how we feel and start relying on the God who fills us. Allow God to lead you today, and if you'll obey, it could change someone's life. It might even change yours!

## PRAYER

*Lord, thank You for choosing to use me to represent You. Help me to trust You and not doubt my unique qualification. Give me a lens that sees opportunities You set before me. In Jesus' name, Amen.*

## WHAT IS THE HOLY SPIRIT SAYING TO ME?

## FOR FURTHER STUDY
2 Corinthians 12:9; Romans 8:37; Hebrews 13:21

DAY 19

# LOVE OVER LEGALISM

By Chelsea Seaton

*Then Jesus said to the crowds and to his disciples, "The teachers of religious law and the Pharisees are the official interpreters of the law of Moses. So practice and obey whatever they tell you, but don't follow their example. For they don't practice what they teach. They crush people with unbearable religious demands and never lift a finger to ease the burden. Everything they do is for show. On their arms they wear extra wide prayer boxes with Scripture verses inside, and they wear robes with extra long tassels."* Matthew 23:1–5 (NLT)

One day while worshipping at church, we sang the lyrics: "Holy are You, God. Holy is Your name." The song was so moving that most every hand went up in praise including mine. As we worshipped together, my eyes were closed, my hands were up, I was belting out the song, and ... thinking about what I'm going to have for dinner: Honey Nut Cheerios or peanut butter and jelly? Now,

on the outside, I'm sure I looked like a great Christian and an in-love-with-Jesus worshipper. Only that's not what was happening in my mind and heart. I was somewhere else thinking about dinner!

If you've been a Christian for any length of time you've probably heard about the Pharisees and how we aren't supposed to be like them. In Matthew's account, Jesus constantly called them out for doing religious acts but with the wrong hearts. It's very easy to judge those mean ol' Pharisees, but the truth is we can all be Pharisees.

We know the churchgoer rules and etiquette. The parts of the song when our hands go up. When to say "Amen" or nod our heads when the speaker says something *tweetable*. We know the don'ts, the dos, and the areas that are approved, depending on your denomination.

Those things are not necessarily wrong. The book of James tells us that our "faith without works is dead," but if you're doing works for show and your heart couldn't care less, then you may have a Pharisee problem.

Jesus says in John 13:35, it's your love that will prove to the world that you are His disciple. He doesn't say it's your good deeds and church attendance that show people you're a Christian. It's love—not legalism.

Your love might cause you to do crazy things like letting someone over in traffic or remaining calm after 45 minutes on hold and not getting what you wanted from the cable company. It may even cause you to see the perspective of someone who votes differently than you. But when we do good works because of Christ's love in our hearts, those works will be fruitful, light, and win people to Him. If we do them out of obligation, it will feel burdensome and be ineffective.

Be effective today. Do awesome things because Christ loves you and you want to offer that same love to others—not because someone is watching or you have a Christian obligation. Choose love over legalism today.

## PRAYER

*Jesus, please forgive me for the times I've done things for the wrong reasons. Please fill me with Your Holy Spirit that I might show Your love to people today. In Jesus' name, Amen.*

## WHAT IS THE HOLY SPIRIT SAYING TO ME?

## FOR FURTHER STUDY
*Romans 14:14–19; Galatians 3:10–14; Isaiah 29:13*

DAY 20

# GOD'S GAME PLAN

*By Kam Hunt*

*For the moment all discipline seems painful rather than pleasant, but later it yields the peaceful fruit of righteousness to those who have been trained by it. Hebrews 12:11 (ESV)*

Years ago, I played football for Texas Christian University, and I loved every minute of it. With up to 40,000 people attending each game, there's no experience quite like hearing the screaming fans, feeling the adrenaline course through your veins, executing the perfect play from coach's game plan, and best of all, *sacking quarterbacks*. When you combine all of that with the possibility of actually winning a game, you can ride the wave of that excitement for weeks!

But before I could ever step onto the field, I had to learn to be disciplined in my pursuit of the game. The most important lesson I learned was if I didn't consistently show up for practice or follow the coach's plan, I wouldn't be prepared to execute in the game.

This lesson doesn't just apply to the football field, it applies to our lives every day as we follow God's game plan. The best thing about His plan is that it always points us to victory, which is a certainty when we follow it. The key for us lies in being disciplined and consistent in learning His Word, studying it, and obeying it no matter what—even when our circumstances make it seem like there's no way to win. And with anything that requires discipline, there are times when it's easy and there are times when you feel like you're going through the motions. However, it's always rewarding. Here's what Hebrews 12:11 says about it: "For the moment all discipline seems painful rather than pleasant, but later it yields the peaceful fruit of righteousness to those who have been trained by it" (ESV).

When we're disciplined about following God's plan for us, we find His victory in our lives. If you haven't discovered His game plan for *your* life, allow me to pour some purpose into you. You were created to worship God, live a life of freedom on earth through the sacrifice of Jesus Christ, and share the good news of what Jesus did. When all seems lost, fall back on those three things, stay diligent in studying the Bible, press through the pain of any personal failures, and remain committed to God's game plan.

## PRAYER

*Lord, thank You for Your Word. Please give me the discipline to follow Your game plan, even when things don't make sense. In Jesus' name, Amen.*

## WHAT IS THE HOLY SPIRIT SAYING TO ME?

## FOR FURTHER STUDY
*1 Corinthians 9:24–27; Proverbs 12:1; Psalm 94:12–14*

*DAY 21*

# WE CAN'T HELP IT

By Jan Greenwood

*"For we cannot but speak the things which we have seen and heard."*

Acts 4:20

I can't pick a tasty watermelon for the life of me. I've failed so many times, it has become a family joke. No matter how many times I stand at the bin, tap on the watermelons, or try to select the perfect one, it most often fails to meet my expectations.

Did you know that watermelons will actually "witness" to you if you pay attention? In desperation one day, I found an article that told me how to look at the stem and markings on the outside of the melon to discern the ripeness inside. It seems that even a watermelon can't help but testify to its experience! It's not only true of watermelons; it's also true of people.

In Matthew 7:16 Jesus said, "You will know them by their fruits." The context around this often-quoted passage cautions us about false prophets. We can lean upon this principle to help us discern the authenticity and validity of another's witness. If we look and listen carefully, we will be able to read and discern the stem and markings of their life. We can see if their fruit is ripe or rotten.

At salvation, the Holy Spirit makes us witnesses. This exchange roots you into the family of God like a stem in soil and begins to mark your life with new identity. It changes who you are. It is neither optional nor mandatory; rather, it is inevitable. Then our ongoing walk with Christ produces fruit that validates the authenticity of our salvation. Our testimony begins to speak and produce salvation in others.

In Acts 4, Peter and John find themselves in a lot of trouble because they've been witnessing to anyone who would listen. Their encounter with the Holy Spirit in Acts 2 filled them with a bold urgency to share what they had seen and heard. Their testimony stirred thousands of people to receive Christ and brought healing to others. This alarmed the local leaders, and soon they were arrested and brought before them to give an account. When told to stop witnessing, Peter responded with a profound revelation: "For we cannot but speak the things which we have seen and heard."

So the next time you are strolling the produce aisle of your local grocery store, remember that your fruit—your testimony—cannot help but speak. If you're full of the Holy Spirit, it's going to show, so why not go ahead and speak boldly about Him? Allow your testimony to be examined. Show the "stem" and "markings" that reveal the inner sweetness of your life so that others might turn to Christ and experience an encounter of their own.

## PRAYER

*Father, I thank You that You have revealed Your son to me and that I bear fruit that speaks to others of Your goodness. I pray You would make me a faithful witness with an abundant testimony of Your saving power. In Jesus' name, Amen.*

## WHAT IS THE HOLY SPIRIT SAYING TO ME?

## FOR FURTHER STUDY
*John 36–39; John 8:13–16, 15:26; Isaiah 43:8–13, 44:6–11; Acts 22:14–16*

# LIFE

*A source of vitality; an animating force; the quality that distinguishes the living from the dead.*

DAY 22

# THE GOOD NEWS ABOUT HELL

*by Mark Jobe*

*"'Depart from me, you who are cursed, into the eternal fire prepared for the devil and his angels.'"* Matthew 25:41 (NIV)

Have you ever had to be the bearer of bad news? It's not very much fun. That's what was on my mind as I thought about what to write on the topic of heaven versus hell. Sure, talking about heaven in an encouraging way is easy, but hell is a different story. In that moment, it was as if the Lord said to me, "Tell them the good news about hell."

"Good news?" I asked.

We learn from Scripture that heaven is a place filled with the overwhelming goodness and glory of God. No more tears, no more pain, no more suffering—only the presence of God and *life*. Heaven is a place where we are reunited with our loved ones, heroes of the faith, and the Lord Himself! On the other hand, hell is a place of darkness, bondage, torment, and eternal fire. Not to mention all of the demons, the devil, and everything evil. That alone is enough to scare the devil out of you! As a loving and caring person who knows the Lord, I would never wish that on anyone.

The reality of hell is a sobering thought. This reality motivates me to be a better witness for Christ. When I think about how many unsaved people are around me every day, I can't help but share the love of Christ with someone. We cannot stand by and do nothing. Lives are being impacted for eternity.

When the early disciples witnessed God's work in the lives of others, according to Acts 4:20, they shared what they saw and heard. When someone's life was changed, they talked about it. When someone was healed or set free, they spread the news. We are called by God to do the same.

So, what is the good news about hell? Not only does it motivate me to be a better witness, but the best news is that *it was never created for us*. Matthew 25:41 says that hell was created for the devil and his angels. Through yielding our lives to Jesus Christ and receiving Him as our Savior and Lord, we are given eternal life. Not only do we escape hell but we can be freed from the powers of hell on earth right now. Our hearts are changed! We are forgiven, set free, and given a new life both here and in heaven. Thank the Lord that we have a choice.

So, ask the Lord to fill you with His loving presence. Make it a point today to share that love with someone else. Tell them the good news that God has saved them from hell by sending His Son to die for our sins. Share your story—bring a little heaven into their life today!

### PRAYER

*God, thank You for rescuing me from hell. Never let me forget that hell is a very real place that people need rescuing from! Help me to bring heaven into someone's life today. In Jesus' name, Amen.*

## WHAT IS THE HOLY SPIRIT SAYING TO ME?

## FOR FURTHER STUDY

*Revelation 21:1-8; Romans 6:23; John 14:1-3*

# DAY 23

# WHAT DO THEY HAVE THAT I DON'T HAVE?

> By Troy Wierman

*"Here's another way to put it: You're here to be light, bringing out the God-colors in the world. God is not a secret to be kept. We're going public with this, as public as a city on a hill. If I make you light-bearers, you don't think I'm going to hide you under a bucket, do you? I'm putting you on a light stand. Now that I've put you there on a hilltop, on a light stand—shine! Keep open house; be generous with your lives. By opening up to others, you'll prompt people to open up with God, this generous Father in heaven." Matthew 5:14–16 (MSG)*

It was a beautiful day at a village in the highlands of Guatemala. Gateway children's ministry and medical teams were busy serving residents inside a local school as construction teams spruced up the walls with new paint. Though it was the end of a physically demanding day, laughter, smiles, and children's worship music saturated the atmosphere.

The founder of the local ministry we were serving grabbed my hand and dragged me to the other side of the courtyard. She took me to an indigenous pastor who was ministering to the residents waiting to see the medical team. I could see he was lovingly praying for and sharing the gospel with the people. He proceeded to tell me the story of how he became a pastor.

Five years earlier, he was an alcoholic and worshipped false gods of the Mayan religion. While stumbling through the streets, he noticed unusual activity at the school. Peering from outside the fence into the courtyard, he saw a group of foreign missionaries genuinely caring for and loving the people of his village. At that moment, he thought, *Why are these people helping my friends with such joy? What do they have that I don't have?*

The way they were ministering to his friends, showing God's light, prompted him to enter the courtyard that day. That's when he discovered what they had was a relationship with the one true God, and that was missing in his life. He ended his story in tears, sharing with us that he recognized several of the Gateway team members as the same people he watched through the fence five years ago.

In the book *Lifestyle Evangelism* by Joe Aldrich, an evangelistic lifestyle "calls Christians to live an attractive, winsome, holy life that captures the attention of neighbors and coworkers to earn a chance to share the gospel."

Living an evangelistic lifestyle makes it easy and natural to form relationships with people that open the door to conversations about what Jesus has done in your life and can do in theirs. To paraphrase Matthew 5:15–16, be a light in your community to attract people. You don't have to be in a foreign country to live evangelistically. In your everyday life, always be ready to give an encouraging word, lend a helping hand, show a smile, and comfort others. When you do these things to glorify God, and not yourself, you're playing a part in fulfilling the Great Commission!

I challenge you to tell others about the Good News of Jesus and live as He lived, filled with the fruit of the Spirit. This is how we can truly live a life of evangelism.

**Holy Spirit, saturate my every action so I can live a lifestyle that attracts others to You. Give me the words to draw people to You and glorify Your name. Tap me on the shoulder when I glorify myself. I want to be a light, and I want to shine for You to prompt others to open up to You. I love You. In Jesus' name, Amen.**

*WHAT IS THE HOLY SPIRIT SAYING TO ME?*

*FOR FURTHER STUDY*

*Romans 1:16, 1 Peter 3:15, Ephesians 4:1–3*

DAY 24

# STEP OUT AND BE A FRIEND

*By Raul Cabrera*

*"This is My commandment, that you love one another as I have loved you. Greater love has no one than this, than to lay down one's life for his friends."* John 15:12–13

The sound of the doorbell rang at my grandmother's house early one morning. It was our neighbor who was on her daily walk and had decided to stop by for a cup of coffee. The problem was, my grandmother was watching her "stories" (soap operas for those not familiar with the moniker). The year was 1989, I was 10 years old, and the DVR had not yet been invented. Though this was an unexpected visit, it was a welcomed one, because my grandmother always made friends a priority, even if it meant missing an episode of *The Young and the Restless.*

It was a different time back then, the world felt friendlier. Sometimes, I find it difficult to make friends in the times we live in today. But even in a world where face-to-face connections have been replaced by apps, snaps, and GIFs, we must make the effort to step out and be a friend.

In John 15:13, Jesus says, "Greater love has no one than this, than to lay down one's life for his friends." In this verse, John uses the Greek word *philos (fee-los)* for "friends," which means a trusted confidant, someone dearly prized in a personal way. This is someone who is more valuable than an acquaintance, a casual friend, or a colleague.

Jesus is a master at making *philos* friends. In Luke 5:1–11, before Jesus called the first disciples, He built a relationship with them. Simon and Andrew, who were expert fishermen, had not caught a single fish that day. In an effort to befriend them, Jesus took them fishing out in the deeper waters where they caught so much fish their boats began to sink.

The strategy was simple. To make friends with Simon and Andrew, Jesus did something with them that they liked to do. He went fishing with fishermen! Jesus was *being a friend* by making what they liked a priority.

Likewise, being a friend means laying down your life or sacrificing your time to do something with or for someone else that they like or enjoy. So, step out and go hunting with someone who likes to hunt or shop with someone who loves weekend flea markets. It's not a waste of your time but a sacrifice of your time toward building *philos* friends—even if it means missing an episode of *The Young and the Restless*.

## PRAYER

**Lord, I thank You for the people in my life, and I pray You help me discover ways to speak joy into their hearts, in Jesus' name, Amen.**

*WHAT IS THE HOLY SPIRIT SAYING TO ME?*

*FOR FURTHER STUDY*
Colossians 3:12–14; Proverbs 17:17

REAL
*LIFE*

DAY 25

# INVESTING IN OTHERS

*By Mark Harris*

*He gives strength to the weary and increases the power of the weak. Even youths grow tired and weary, and young men stumble and fall; but those who hope in the Lord will renew their strength. They will soar on wings like eagles; they will run and not grow weary, they will walk and not be faint. Isaiah 40:29–31 (NIV)*

Most of us have probably heard Warren Buffet's quote, "The best investment you will ever make is in yourself." It may seem selfish and counterintuitive to Christian advice, but did you know it's actually extremely biblical to invest in yourself, so you are able to invest in others?

Jesus set a great example as He lived on earth. In Matthew 11:28–30 (MSG), He calls this the "unforced rhythms of grace": "Come to me. Get away with me and you'll recover your life. I'll show you how to take a real rest. Walk with me and work with me—watch how I do it. Learn the unforced rhythms of grace. I won't lay anything heavy or ill-fitting on you. Keep company with me and you'll learn to live freely and lightly."

If you want to be able to invest in others and make a difference in their lives, you must first invest in yourself. Jesus was always investing in others. He was constantly pouring out. In just one very busy day, Jesus went from preaching in the synagogue to casting out a demon, healing a sick friend, and at sundown, ministering to the entire city gathered at His door (Mark 1:21–34).

But what always preceded or followed His times of pouring out was a time away. Time spent investing in Himself. Time praying, listening, and refueling. In Mark 1:35 (ESV), following His busy day, we see that "very early in the morning, while it was still dark, he departed and went out to a desolate place and there he prayed."

Jesus also invited His disciples into His unforced rhythm of grace. In Mark 6:31–32 (ESV), "And he said to them, 'Come away by yourselves to a desolate place and rest a while.' For many were coming and going, and they had no leisure even to eat."

To pour into others, we need to be equipped with something to give. And the way we have something to give is to rest spiritually, physically, and mentally. You can't pour anything out of an empty container. Are you investing in yourself daily and spending time with the Lord? Are you regularly investing in your soul so that you can invest in other people?

## PRAYER

*(Prayer of St. Francis)*

*Lord, make me an instrument of Your peace.*
*Where there is hatred, let me bring love.*
*Where there is offense, let me bring pardon.*
*Where there is discord, let me bring union.*
*Where there is error, let me bring truth.*
*Where there is doubt, let me bring faith.*
*Where there is despair, let me bring hope.*
*Where there is darkness, let me bring Your light.*
*Where there is sadness, let me bring joy.*

*O Master, let me not seek as much*
*to be consoled as to console,*
*to be understood as to understand,*
*to be loved as to love,*
*for it is in giving that one receives,*
*it is in self-forgetting that one finds,*
*it is in pardoning that one is pardoned,*
*it is in dying that one is raised to eternal life.*

## WHAT IS THE HOLY SPIRIT SAYING TO ME?

_____

_____

_____

_____

_____

_____

_____

_____

_____

_____

_____

_____

_____

_____

_____

_____

_____

_____

_____

_____

## FOR FURTHER STUDY

Jeremiah 31:25, Romans 12:1–2, Psalm 51:10

# DAY 26

# SMALL ACTS OF BIG FAITH

by Marcus Brecheen

*After this I looked, and there before me was a great multitude that no one could count, from every nation, tribe, people and language, standing before the throne and before the Lamb. They were wearing white robes and were holding palm branches in their hands. And they cried out in a loud voice: "Salvation belongs to our God, who sits on the throne, and to the Lamb."* Revelation 7:9–10 (NIV)

In late eighteenth-century England, there was a man named William Carey who had a level of faith and selflessness that I aspire to. He and a group of men met regularly to pray, and they genuinely believed their prayers were connected to God's work on earth. They were all stirred by the Gospel and its power to save. During one of these prayer meetings, they began talking about India and its need for the Gospel message. Each of the men had a burden, and Carey compared it to standing at the entrance of a cavernous mine that had never been explored. He stood up and said to the other men, "I will go down if you will hold the rope."

In April 1793, Carey set sail for India, and today he is known as the father of modern missions having translated the Bible into 44 different languages. It all started in a small prayer group, and God shook a big nation.

Carey held up his end of the deal, and his friends did too—every day for the rest of their lives! Together by faith, they said "yes" to God's invitation to India.

But what about those men back home? Do you think they ever considered *praying* for Carey to be too simple an act—inadequate compared to his work of actually *going*? I wonder if they ever had days when they felt useless. The truth is it can be easy to believe what we do has little or no impact on the world. Not only is this wrong thinking but also a lack of faith. It's also the beginning of selfishness, which leads you down a path that says, "If my life doesn't matter anyway, I may as well give up and get comfortable." And so begins the plunge into doing whatever we want because we don't think it will affect anyone. This is small thinking that views God as selfish, distant, and uncaring.

But what if our lives—our choices, prayers, worship, integrity, and willingness to live by faith—really do matter? Even if our lives seem small and our impact in God's kingdom seems insignificant, we are connected to God's big work on earth. We have a major role to play no matter how big or small. William Carey and his friends believed it. Only God knows the ruin that marks the earth today, and only God sees how the antidote will be administered. Whether it be through the simple act of prayer or altering your life to follow God's call, He has an invitation for you today. All it requires is faith that the small thing we do connects to the big thing God is doing. What is God calling you to do today?

## PRAYER

*God, give us faith today to make the connection between what You're doing and what we do. You spoke life and earth into being, and You have set Your people on a great mission. Thank You for people throughout history who saw their lives—when connected to Yours—as worthy of offering as a living sacrifice. Give us grace to do so today. In Jesus' name, Amen.*

## WHAT IS THE HOLY SPIRIT SAYING TO ME?

## FOR FURTHER STUDY
*Revelation 5; Hebrews 11; Matthew 25:31-40*

DAY 27

# THE GREATEST GIFT YOU CAN GIVE THE NEXT GENERATION

*by Sion Alford*

*And a voice came from heaven: "You are my Son, whom I love; with you I am well pleased."* Luke 3:22 (NIV)

The water moved swiftly beneath His calloused, Galilean feet. A chill ran up His back as He stepped further into the cool river to join His eccentric friend and cousin, John, who insisted, "You should be baptizing *me*!"

"No, the time has come. The waiting is over," answered the Nazarene. "It should be done, for we must carry out all that my Father requires."

As He rose from the Jordan River's water the heavens suddenly opened and the Spirit of God descended on Jesus like a dove. Then *it* happened. The silence of heaven was interrupted. A voice broke through the stillness of time with the sound of thunder. Jesus knew the voice behind the rumble. He recognized the thunderous applause from heaven as His Father's loving voice.

"This is my beloved Son, in whom I am well pleased!"

Jesus heard words of affirmation and not commands like "Go here!" or "Do this!" He heard words of *identity* that spoke to who He was, not what He had done. They were exactly what this waiting Savior needed to hear after 30 long years of preparation.

No miracles had been performed. No healings had been demonstrated. No sermons had been preached. Only obedient obscurity. God broke through the silence of Jesus' journey and confirmed the true *identity* of His Son.

The best gift we can give our children (and the next generation) is our affirmation of their true *identity*. Just as Jesus was not fully prepared for ministry until He had received the affirmation of His heavenly Father, we must realize that our children need the same before they are sent into the world to fulfill His will. Everything they face during their hiddenness in your home is to prepare them for their calling. It is during this season of their lives that we, as parents, are to teach, train, and prepare them for *who* they are and *whose* they are.

What does this look like in practical terms? If you are a parent, read the Word of God with your children. Pray with your children. Teach them to hear His voice. Prophesy and declare His promises over them. Even if you aren't a parent, you can live out the call to raise up the next generation too. We are all surrounded by people younger than we are, and we have the ability to mentor them and affirm their identity. One day they will step into the Jordan River of their life prepared to fulfill their destiny and calling. Let the thunderous applause of heaven fill their hearts as they recite the affirmation of their Father in heaven: "I am a child of God!"

### PRAYER

*Heavenly Father, thank You for giving me the identity of being Your child. Thank You for the times You have hidden me, so I could learn who I am and whose I am. Help me to be a good role model to the next generation and help me to teach them about their true identity in You. In Jesus' name, Amen.*

## WHAT IS THE HOLY SPIRIT SAYING TO ME?

## FOR FURTHER STUDY

*Galatians 3:25–27, 4:6–7; 2 Corinthians 5:17*

# DAY 28

# DOING OUR PART

By Robert Morris

*He who sows sparingly will also reap sparingly, and he who sows bountifully will also reap bountifully. So let each one give as he purposes in his heart, not grudgingly or of necessity; for God loves a cheerful giver. And God is able to make all grace abound toward you, that you, always having all sufficiency in all things, may have an abundance for every good work.* 2 Corinthians 9:6–8

When my father was 16 years old, my grandfather (his father) had a job with the department of transportation filling potholes with asphalt. He worked alongside a Christian man named Ray Alexander who shared the gospel with him. One day, Ray invited my grandfather over to his house after dinner to share more about Jesus. As my grandfather walked out the door to meet Ray, my father asked if he could drive him. My grandfather agreed to let him drive but told him he had to wait outside Ray's house.

While Ray was sharing the gospel with my grandfather, my dad was sitting outside on the front porch and because there was no air conditioning back then, the door was open and my dad could hear everything. It was the first time my dad ever heard anyone talk about the gospel. At the end of their conversation, Ray asked my grandfather if he wanted to accept Jesus as his Savior, but he said no.

Then Ray said, "If you ever decide you want to get saved, pray a prayer like this." As he recited the prayer, my father prayed along with him and accepted Jesus. Because my father was saved, I grew up in a Christian home where the gospel was planted in my life, and now *thousands* of people have come to know Jesus through the ministry of Gateway Church. And it all started with one man's obedience to share the gospel.

This story depicts an amazing kingdom principle: *you reap more than you sow.* Think about it for a moment. When a farmer plants a single kernel of corn, the kernel will grow into a stalk that will produce hundreds of kernels. 2 Corinthians 9:6 says, "He who sows bountifully will also reap bountifully." But just before that it says, "He who sows sparingly will also reap sparingly." It's amazing to me that people expect to reap a huge harvest of souls when they haven't planted the seed of the gospel. The truth is, it's our only job. We share the Good News, and God takes care of the results. Even if you lead just a few people to the Lord over your lifetime, you might never know the impact you'll have on the kingdom of God.

Several years ago, when my grandfather was very old, I led him to the Lord—45 years *after* Ray Alexander planted the seed. I called Ray and told him the story about my father accepting Christ that day at his house and about how my grandfather had recently given his life to Jesus. When I finished telling him the story, he said, "I have the name of every person I've ever shared the gospel with written down in the back of my Bible. When they get saved, I put a check beside their name. Your grandfather's name is the only one without a check, but when I get off the phone I'm going to add one."

God has called each of us to plant the seed, and there are people everywhere who need to hear the gospel. If you ever feel like you're not qualified to be a witness, remember this story about a man who poured asphalt into potholes and shared the gospel with everyone he met. Because he sowed bountifully, he has reaped bountifully.

I want to challenge you today to share the gospel bountifully. We just need to do our part and let God do the rest.

*Lord, I want to sow the seed of the gospel as much as possible. Help me to see opportunities to plant seeds in people's lives, and help me to live a lifestyle of evangelism. In Jesus' name, Amen.*

## WHAT IS THE HOLY SPIRIT SAYING TO ME?

## FOR FURTHER STUDY

*Isaiah 55:11; Mark 4:26–29*

REAL SERIES GROUPS
DISCUSSION GUIDE

# WEEK 1

**RELEVANT: Having obvious significance upon; pertinent; or relating to the matter at hand.**

We are called to be relevant fishers of people. Jesus said, "Follow Me, and I will make you fishers of men."

## READ

**Matthew 4:18–22**

And Jesus, walking by the Sea of Galilee, saw two brothers, Simon called Peter, and Andrew his brother, casting a net into the sea; for they were fishermen. Then He said to them, "Follow Me, and I will make you fishers of men." They immediately left their nets and followed Him. Going on from there, He saw two other brothers, James the son of Zebedee, and John his brother, in the boat with Zebedee their father, mending their nets. He called them, and immediately they left the boat and their father, and followed Him.

## DISCUSS

Notice that Jesus didn't choose preachers to be His disciples. He chose normal, everyday, working people. Pastor Robert has said that everyday people can make an even greater impact for the kingdom than preachers. *Do you believe that is true? Why or why not?*

Any story about God's goodness is bait on a hook that we can throw out. *Who has a story about God's goodness they would be willing to share?*

_____

_____

_____

Oftentimes we believe for a testimony to be relevant or impactful it has to be about living an immoral life and then being radically saved. *Have you ever felt like your salvation story isn't good enough? Have you been able to share it anyway or not?*

_____

_____

_____

If we're going to be fishers of people, we have to "fish" in the right places, meaning we can't catch fish at church. We have to go where there are unbelievers. *Where can you start fishing tomorrow?*

_____

_____

_____

_____

### PRAYER

**Ask the Holy Spirit to bring to mind the relevant story of God's goodness He wants you to share. Ask Him for the courage to share it in the places where you can go "fishing."**

### ACTION

*Practice sharing your story in under one minute. You can practice with a trusted friend, spouse, or alone in your car.*

# WEEK 2

In week one, Jesus uses fishing for people as an analogy, and in Matthew, Jesus doesn't use an analogy. He says we *are* light, and we *are* salt.

## READ

### Matthew 5:13–16

"You are the salt of the earth; but if the salt loses its flavor, how shall it be seasoned? It is then good for nothing but to be thrown out and trampled underfoot by men. You are the light of the world. A city that is set on a hill cannot be hidden. Nor do they light a lamp and put it under a basket, but on a lampstand, and it gives light to all who are in the house. Let your light so shine before men, that they may see your good works and glorify your Father in heaven."

## DISCUSS

Salt and light both are influential. Salt influences flavor, and light influences darkness. *Where do you have a hard time being salt and light? What makes it difficult, and what can you do to overcome the difficulty?*

Psalm 34 says, "taste and see that the Lord is good." If we are salt then we are giving the world its taste of God. *Examine your life. What are some areas where you can give a better taste of God's goodness?*

_____

_____

_____

We are light in a dark world and can influence the dark around us by letting our light shine. *Who can share a testimony of being light in a dark place?*

_____

_____

_____

When we share the light in us, we can win people to Christ. *Where can you let your light shine tomorrow?*

_____

_____

_____

## PRAYER

**Ask the Holy Spirit to reveal the areas where He wants to heal, so you can give a good flavor to those around you. Ask Him to help you be the light in your workplace, home, and community.**

## ACTION

Write down one place where you want to be a salt and light influence this week, and write one practical way you can do that.

# WEEK 3

*AUTHENTIC: Genuine; real; trustworthy; reliable; that which can be believed or accepted; not counterfeit or false; true to its type.*

We are all called to be witnesses. Sometimes we think to witness we must have the right education and experience, but all we need to share is what we've seen and heard.

## READ

### Acts 1:4–8

And being assembled together with them, He commanded them not to depart from Jerusalem, but to wait for the Promise of the Father, "which," He said, "you have heard from Me; for John truly baptized with water, but you shall be baptized with the Holy Spirit not many days from now." Therefore, when they had come together, they asked Him, saying, "Lord, will You at this time restore the kingdom to Israel?" And He said to them, "It is not for you to know times or seasons which the Father has put in His own authority. But you shall receive power when the Holy Spirit has come upon you; and you shall be witnesses to Me in Jerusalem, and in all Judea and Samaria, and to the end of the earth."

## DISCUSS

A witness is someone who communicates their experiences. And as Christians that means sharing something God has done in our lives. Yet many times we plead the fifth and resist sharing our story. *Why has it been hard to share your story?*

In Luke 7:22, Jesus tells John's disciples to go tell him what they have seen and heard. *Can someone share a story of something they have seen or heard God do in their life?*

When you think about a courtroom, there are witnesses, lawyers, and a judge. We are called to be the witness, not the lawyer or judge. *Do you ever find it hard to be the witness instead of the judge? Would anyone share a time lately that it was difficult?*

If we're going to witness, we have to go where the people are and seize opportunities to share our stories. *Besides the workplace, where are some places you can seize opportunities to witness?*

## PRAYER

**Ask the Holy Spirit to help you share your story, and highlight times when you need to seize the opportunity to share.**

## ACTION

*Share your story with at least one person this week.*

**LIFE: A source of vitality; an animating force; the quality that distinguishes the living from the dead.**

Sowing and reaping is a life principle, not just a financial one. Sowing is simply sharing the gospel and what God has done in our lives. When we sow seeds of the gospel, God will do the rest.

## READ

### 2 Corinthians 9:6
But this I say: He who sows sparingly will also reap sparingly, and he who sows bountifully will also reap bountifully.

## DISCUSS

According to this passage, we reap what we sow. Sometimes we expect to win people to Jesus, but we aren't sowing seeds. If we just start sowing, we'll reap souls. *What has kept you from "sowing seeds"?*

1 Corinthians 3:4–6 explains that we plant seeds, but God gives the increase. As Pastor Robert explained, it's not our responsibility to win people to Christ. That is God's responsibility. *Have you ever felt like it's your responsibility to win people to Christ and then felt disappointed if you didn't?*

Satan wants you to feel like a failure if you don't win a person to Christ after planting the seed, but you are not a failure. *Can you share a time when you shared the gospel, but the person didn't receive Christ? What were your thoughts and how did you feel?*

If we keep planting seeds of the gospel, we will reap more than we sow. You never know who the person you witness to is going to tell, and who they'll tell, and before you know it hundreds or thousands of people know Christ because of one seed. *Does anyone have a success story of planting a seed and seeing God do more?*

## PRAYER

**Ask the Holy Spirit to help you be a life-giving farmer and plant the seed of the gospel everywhere you go.**

## ACTION

Plant the seed of the gospel to at least one person this week.

*MEMORY VERSES*